DIONE

In memory of a mother much loved

Doris J Wakefield

Dione
Copyright © 2019 by Doris J Wakefield

All rights reserved. No part of this publication may be reproduced, distributed, or transmitted in any form or by any means, including photocopying, recording, or other electronic or mechanical methods, without the prior written permission of the author, except in the case of brief quotations embodied in critical reviews and certain other non-commercial uses permitted by copyright law.

Tellwell Talent
www.tellwell.ca

ISBN
978-0-2288-1120-6 (Hardcover)
978-0-2288-1119-0 (Paperback)

Table of Contents

Dedication vii
Acknowledgements. ix
Prologue. xi

Chapter 1: Moose Jaw 1
Chapter 2: Education. 5
Chapter 3: Married Life 6
Chapter 4: Life on the Farm at Lewvan, Saskatchewan 9
Chapter 5: Golf School. 12
Chapter 6: Childhood Capers 13
Chapter 7: Jack Lehr 16
Chapter 8: Fun and Games 19
Chapter 9: Ifield School Days. 21
Chapter 10: Neighbours. 25
Chapter 11: Where Love Resides 27
Chapter 12: Always a Mom, Always a Teacher 29
Chapter 13: The Family in Crisis. 33
Chapter 14: Arriving in Chauvin 37
Chapter 15: Home at the Hutterite Colony 40
Chapter 16: Teaching Assignment at Sydenham School 45
Chapter 17: Life in Edgerton, Alberta 48

Epilogue. 57
About The Author 65

Edith Dione Cross at eighteen years old as she graduated from her teachers' training at Moose Jaw Normal School

Dedication

In Memory of the Life of Dione
a courageous woman
wife, mother, grandmother

This is a family story based on real facts and written fifty-six years after our mom went to her eternal rest.

This book reveals the highs and the lows of the life of an amazing mother as she handled life events with fortitude and a dignity that most of us can never imagine.

It's a story of a mother's unending gift of unconditional love. This book is dedicated to the memory of my mother, a shy, gentle woman of faith. She lived her life with intent and unconditional love.

Doris Wakefield
&
Donald Lehr

Acknowledgements

To my brother, Don, who shared my life, for his support and amazing memory of the past that brought chuckles and flooded my mind with memories of our childhood. These memories helped to complete this dedication to our mom.

To my niece, Charlene Brown, for her initial attempt to organize my writing.

To my niece, Connie McMann, for her recording skills as Don and I travelled down memory lane for six hours one day.

To my family and all the people who endured my constant reminder that "I'm writing this book" as they waited in silent anticipation for its completion.

To my family of origin for all the love and care that I received throughout my life.

To my husband, Charles, who lovingly supported me in life and even now.

Lastly, to my adult children for giving me purpose and sometimes challenges.

Thank you!

Dione and Arthur in England as their parents left for Canada. They appear confused and scared, even though they were promised that Momma and Daddy would send for them in one year. This promise was kept.

Prologue

Blackburn, England

Six-year-old Dione, with her dark curly locks and hazel eyes, stares out from beneath a bright knit tam. She is standing at the dock looking at a huge ship in the harbour of London. She stands stiffly beside her Grandma Cross and four-year-old brother Arthur. She stands watching Momma and Daddy as they walk up the gangplank of the big ship and disappear from her sight.

Dione still feels the warm tight hug of her momma as she tells her, "You're a big girl now and I need you to look after your brother until I can send for you." Dione sees Momma wipe away the tears that flood her face and she feels Momma's heart beating hard.

She remembers Daddy's words as he hugs her and in his stern father voice says to her, "Dione, you be a good girl and mind what Grandma says now." Then Grandma takes her hand and they walk away.

Dione glances back and she is puzzled; where are Momma and Daddy going? Where is that place far away in Canada that they talked about just yesterday? Why aren't they taking Arthur and me with them?

Dione loves her Grandma though and she tries to be good all the time. She looks out for her little brother and tries to keep him from getting into mischief and making Grandma mad, but sometimes it is hard because he is so curious about every little thing and he is cheeky too. Sometimes she goes in her room and cries into her pillow as Arthur receives his discipline.

CHAPTER ONE

Moose Jaw

Edith Dione Cross was born at 17 Whittaker Street, Blackburn County, England in 1907. She was the eldest child of Walter and Cecelia Cross.

In 1913, when she was seven years old, she came to Wolf Street, Moose Jaw, Saskatchewan where her parents had settled one year previous.

Dione's father, Walter Fredrick Cross, joined the Canadian Army and was injured in action at Vimy Ridge April 14, 1917 during World War I. He passed away on board a ship, leaving Dione's mother a pregnant widow with three young children.

Dione would have a lot of responsibility caring her siblings in the years ahead as her mother worked at various domestic jobs including YMCA in Moose Jaw where she served for many years until her retirement. During this time, Grandma Cross received a war widow's pension. Grandma Cross often spoke of "her boys" at the "Y" with great warmth.

A short story of Grandma Cross has been recorded in a separate document called "At the very Sole of Bridgette." It contains some family secrets and will be made available to family members.

Grandma Cross was eventually able to gather funds for a down payment and purchase a permanent home for her growing family. The home was at 926 Staticona East in Moose Jaw. Many family events took place at that home over the years, including the trousseau tea and wedding reception for Dione's sister Mary.

A special event for this family, as told many years later by Aunty Mary, was the children's birthdays. They were important and celebrated in a special way. The birthday child was provided a dedicated glass bowl to take across to the general store and receive scoops of ice cream for each child. This treat was then brought home to be shared among the siblings.

This special glass bowl was called the "Ice Cream Bowl."

The special glass bowl was given to my daughter Barbara Sjoquist. Some years ago, while recording Aunty Mary's childhood experiences, the story of the ice cream bowl came up. Barbara learned that Grandma Cross had kept the bowl until her death when Aunty Mary took possession of it. Aunty Mary kept it safe until just the right time to pass it to Barbara and a new generation for safe-keeping.

The ice cream bowl recently held several scoops of French vanilla ice cream for my eightieth birthday celebration in December 2016.

M Gmail  Doris Wakefield <djemerald2@gmail.com>

The Ice Cream Bowl #1
1 message

Lennis & Barb Sjoquist <sjoquist@cciwireless.ca>   Thu, Jan 10, 2019 at 10:57 AM
To: Mom <djemerald2@gmail.com>

Morning Mom,

Sending you 3 pictures of the Ice Cream Bowl. It measures 2 1/2" tall by 7 1/2" wide. Our family always uses the Ice Cream Bowl for our family celebrations – it might not always have ice cream in it, but it is on our table and the story of the bowl is repeated. We love sharing the story with friends and family. This little bowl is probably not worth much in the eyes of anyone else, but to me it represents all the goodness and celebrations of our family history. Each time we have it on our table (which was Grandmas table), it reminds me of my family history, of the women who have gone before me, of their strength, their tenacity and their faith. I photographed it on Grandmas table.

I have to send the pictures in 3 separate emails because the resolution is so high.

Love you,
Barb

When I asked Barbara to send me a picture of
this glass bowl, this is the email she sent me with
the picture of the "Ice Cream Bowl."

CHAPTER TWO

EDUCATION

All of Dione's schooling was taken in Moose Jaw, including the normal school where she received a first-class teaching certificate in 1928.

Upon graduation, the normal school offered internship teaching positions in isolated locations in Saskatchewan and this is where Dione began her teaching career.

According to the contract offers she kept among her papers, she taught at the following schools:

Dunkerley SD 2980 - 6 mos. from May 1st, 1926 @ $900
West Lake SD 1536 - January 10th 1927 till notice @ $5day
Garrett SD 3939 - 96 days – Aug 15th till Dec 1929 @ $1000
Cross SD 2188 - 6 mos. from Jan 1930 @ $1300
Cross SD 2188 – Feb 1st, 1931 @ $1100

Her life in these areas exposed her to a new, sometimes harsh life on the prairies where wild berry bushes and wild animals were plentiful and raw land-breaking was common, as were family outings, horseback riding, country dances, and the harsh cold of Saskatchewan winters. Dione told her children stories of these times when she boarded with families in the communities where she taught, and it all seemed very exciting and glamorous to us.

CHAPTER THREE

MARRIED LIFE

In September of 1930, while teaching at Cross School and earning about $900 per year, Dione met John Lehr, an American citizen and local mechanic. They were married on December 24th, 1930 at St Barnabas Church in Moose Jaw, the same church she had attended as a child. Dione continued teaching at Cross school when they returned from their wedding.

The following spring, the couple took up farming a quarter section of rented land and living in an old farmhouse: Section 10, twp. 4, range 17, NW of 2nd Riceton, Saskatchewan.

By December of 1932, after nearly two years of marriage, there was still no pregnancy. While back in Moosejaw visiting family, Jack heard that there was a home where children could be adopted. He went there and found a little boy sitting by himself and looking very sad. The story I was told went like this. Dad went home to Mom and coaxed her to come see him. Mom was a little resistant at first, but after visiting and hearing this little boy's story, they decided to apply to adopt him. He was just under six months old.

From my research, I found that homes for unwed mothers were established by charitable organizations for this purpose in most cities across the country. Since society in 1932 did not accept unwed mothers and girls, they were often sent away by their families to give birth and were often compelled to place the child for adoption.

There was a home requirement for the mother to remain in the home after the birth to work and pay for their stay there. They were encouraged to nurse their baby for three to six months in the interests of a healthy baby. During this time, mother and baby would develop a strong bond. I can only imagine the abandonment these babies must have experienced when their time together ended, and I believe that would have been the reason for Earl's lost and lonely appearance at five months when Mom and Dad adopted him.

Mom never wanted to talk about Earl's adoption because she loved him and felt that he was their child. Aunty Mary, who was Mom's sister and confident, shared information with us later that Mom didn't talk about Earl's adoption because she always felt sad that while she could remember the births of her other children, she could not remember Earl's birth. Aunty Mary later shared other secrets about Earl's birth with me. Earl's birth mother was an unwed mother said to be in a relationship with a married man and that was all the information that was provided because Mom did not want to know anything further. No health information, no heritage information.

Jack and Dione settled in with their little boy. Dione stopped teaching and became a stay-at-home mom.

What a surprise when they discovered they were pregnant after all and Donald John was born in June 1935. Doris Jean was born in December 1936; Russell Fredrick was born in April 1938; and in January 1941, Roger William was born in Regina. (A few years later, in 1946, Gordon Douglas completed the family when we were living in Lewvan.)

Neither Don nor I have much memory of our time at Riceton, although we did travel back there to a local home where we had long ago received our childhood inoculations.

Don recalls a family (the Deeks) that had twins and a son who was killed overseas. Mom and Dad agreed to allow Don stay with them for a while for comfort as they recovered from their grief.

Wedding picture. Wedding date: Dec 24th, 1929 in Moose Jaw Saskatchewan. Attendants were Dione's sister Mary and brothers Arthur and William.

CHAPTER FOUR

LIFE ON THE FARM AT LEWVAN, SASKATCHEWAN

John and Dione relocated their family in 1944 to a quarter section of rented land close to Lewvan, Saskatchewan.

I went with Mom and Katie, the hired girl, to look over the house we would be moving into. It was an old two-storey house that had been vacant for a quite a while, so it was dusty and barren. It was here that Mom set about to make a new home for her family.

The door to the house entered directly into the lean-to kitchen. The linoleum was old and worn. The coal-burning kitchen range with a warming oven and a tank sat on the side that held water. In the corner was a single large porcelain sink set in a makeshift cupboard with the storage doors swinging loose on one set of hinges. There was also a built-in cupboard that stored pots and pans and miscellaneous foodstuff. Kitchen curtains were sewn to cover the one window in the kitchen. Mom later added a kitchen table and chairs and a large kitchen cabinet that stored a selection of everyday dinner dishes and cutlery. The bins in the lower section of the cabinet held flour and sugar, and a hand-turned milk separator took its place among the kitchen fixtures.

The dining room and sitting area were an open space with only the furniture defining them. In the dining area there was a large round oak table and chairs as well as a glass-door china cabinet where crystal glasses and bowls and fancy dishes found their home. A large oak buffet topped with a mirror had extra storage for linens. One drawer held household hardware and the other stored scribblers, crayons, pens, pencils, and other essentials for the comfortable daily lives of our family.

The living or sitting area housed Dad's leather armchair, a large cabinet, a battery-operated radio, and a floral covered Winnipeg couch. I have never seen another Winnipeg couch, but I think it can best be described as a single bed with a mattress. There were extensions on both sides that opened out to make a double bed. Our Winnipeg couch offered a sitting area by day and a bed by night if required.

Mom sewed the window coverings that were a chintz grey fabric with a large floral design. Regular roller blinds were installed but seldom closed.

Soon after moving in, the walls and ceilings were spruced up with fresh wallpaper that mom and Katie applied with a water and flour paste.

The second floor of the house held a bedroom for me and a bedroom for Mom and Dad. In the first year, Mr. Kergan, from Regina, lived with us while he was busy transforming the open sun porch off the living area into a single large bedroom for the boys. A large dresser and two double beds completed the furnishings.

Our property at Lewvan was the centre of the world we knew since it was located just ten miles west of Riceton, ten miles north-east to Sedley, ten miles south-east to Francis, and seven miles south to Lewvan (our mailing address). The city of Regina was an hour north of our farm if you were travelling the average speed of forty-two miles per hour.

Tradition

A family Christmas tradition was making candy. Each child was allowed to choose the type of candy they wanted to make and then we were responsible to either team up with another sibling or conscript Mom to help. Of course, Mom wasn't far away during this candy-making process. Some of the pan candy favourites were chocolate fudge, brown sugar fudge, hard red-coloured crystal candy, butterscotch, and taffy. Not all the projects were a success, but I recall it being a lot of fun and something to look forward to.

Baking was a big event at Christmas. We had a large batch of Christmas fruitcake, rich with candied fruits and nuts. It was supposed to be allowed to cure for several weeks in tight container cans. However, it always seemed to be Christmas Eve when Mom was making the fruitcake and I don't recall that it lasted very long. I have heard of people not liking fruitcake, but I don't understand that. It is one of my favourites. Dad always brought a gallon jug of sherry home for Mom at Christmas which she would use to make her moist fruitcake. Mom also liked a glass of sherry on special occasions, and we saw her enjoying this treat through the years.

Mom kept this drug well out of the reach of the children, or so she thought. One day I found the jug sitting on her dresser in her bedroom and took a sip or two, which made me very sick. Thereafter the jug disappeared to some secure hiding spot.

I have heard that some families didn't observe the Santa Claus fable, believing that it is deceptive. I never saw any sign among my siblings or my cousins that we were harmed by this secret little innocent belief in Santa. Our parents did believe in the Santa Claus tradition and this was a big event, creating great excitement and anticipation in the weeks leading up to Christmas Eve.

CHAPTER FIVE

GOLF SCHOOL

Earl and Don had Welsh ponies. They started attending school at Golf school in the fall after we moved to Lewvan, approximately a five-mile ride. They travelled together until Earl became very unhappy at this school and he went to live with Grandma in Moose Jaw for the rest of that school year. I was then conscripted to ride with Don since Don didn't like school anyway and didn't want to go by himself.

As we rode off to school, Don informed me that we need not force the horses to go too fast lest we tire them out. We patiently brought them to a slow walk the whole distance. While we had started out on time, we arrived just in time for morning recess. I didn't question his instructions; after all, he was my big brother and I was okay with it.

There were no extra desks at the school and I was an unexpected guest, so I had to sit with Don at his desk. Davie Miller sat down across the aisle from us and started to tease me. I had already had a tiring day and recall that I verbally gave him a piece of my mind. This was a talent that I learned quite young, experience gained from living with my brothers.

Don was a master at finding ways to avoid school. One day, as he stopped by before school at the neighbours' house to meet the kids there, he treated his horse to water at the trough. It seems the horse reacted to something and Don *says* the horse kicked him. Since he thought he might be injured, he was unable to carry on to school and he spent the day at the neighbours' house. Don doesn't think Mom knew about. I think Mom knew about it, but she accepted it as another one of Don's manoeuvres to avoid school.

CHAPTER SIX

CHILDHOOD CAPERS

Unlike Mom, Dad didn't have patience and wasn't always sympathetic to our childhood antics. Don recalls getting ready to ride one day but the horse had other ideas and refused to move. Dad gave the horse a slap on the rump and the horse took off, much to Don's surprise.

Mom wasn't much of a disciplinarian, and there were times when one of us went just a bit too far. Don recalls Mom chasing him because of one of those times. He hid under the bed. Not to be outwitted this easily, she grabbed the broom and fished him out to face the music.

Russ and I recall the time we went to the neighbours' house instead of coming home straight after school. As we tried to hide upstairs, Mom dealt with us quickly by persuading us that we should take our punishment now, a few quick smacks on our behinds, rather than wait for Dad to deal with us.

Apparently, Don at one time was a cookie thief, and as he ran out of the house to hide, he bumped into a large scythe that was hanging on an outside wall. As it fell, it cut his fingers. He says he has the scars on his hand to show for this even after these many years.

We always had horses on the farm. We rode them to school and over to the neighbours' house. We rode mostly bareback, although I think there was a saddle on the farm. I know I thought the hardest part of riding was getting the bridle on the horse. Usually one of the boys was handy to do that. The horses had such big teeth and I truthfully was afraid, no matter how I tried to feel comfortable around these huge beasts. While mom had ridden horses as a young school teacher before she was married, we never saw her ride. My dad was quite old fashioned, and I suspect he didn't see horseback riding as ladylike.

Despite my fear, I was determined to ride (because the boys did). I always thought it would be great to have been a boy. They seemed to have so much more fun. One of the things the boys could do that I wasn't supposed to do was ride horseback on my own. I had a vision of riding carefree across the fields on the back of a fast horse.

I think I was about ten when one of my brothers, probably Don or Russ, helped me bridle up our wild little Shetland stallion and I took off for the ride of my life. Billy took the bit in his mouth and I hung on for my life. Finally, Billy had enough and headed for home and the barn. I recall tearing through the yard as we approached the barn and seeing my dad running to rescue me. His words as he rescued me from the ground are still clear to me today: "Stay off that horse until you learn to ride."

We also used a horse to pull the toboggan in the winter. On one such occasion, Earl was riding the horse that was pulling the toboggan. As we slowed down to turn into the driveway, Russ and I tumbled off. One of the neighbours, Davey Miller, was riding behind and unable to stop before his horse ran right over Russ and me. Mom and Dad were watching from the house and they rushed out and picked up Russ and checked him all over. As I followed them to the house, I began to feel pain and Mom turned to see me and realized that I had been hurt. The horse's hoof had grazed my cheekbone. While there were no scars and no bleeding, it could have been so much worse. I'm pretty sure Davey got in deep trouble for riding so close.

We had many favourite games that we played around about the farm. We would play tag and hide and seek well into the later evening after the sun had set.

In winter, the Saturday night bath was a time of interest. It would start early in the day. The boys would gather the clean snow in the round metal tub and it would be melted on the wood stove. Once it was melted and the temperature carefully tested by Mom, the bathing would begin. Youngest first.

I remember being responsible for assisting with the baby's bath and feeling very grown up for being given that responsibility. Gordie and Roger first, then I was given the honoured privilege of bathing next.

I'm not sure of the logic of that, but it was generally accepted that I went next because I was the girl. The boys would have to clear out from the area before their turns: Russell, then Don, and then Earl. Each of us in turn was reminded by Mom not to pee in the bath water.

At some time during the bathing routine there would be additional warm water added from a kettle on the stove.

I recall sometimes when the baths were finished the water would be used to scrub the kitchen floor or to soak the men's overalls. Later, when I was married and didn't yet have a washing machine, I used the baby's bath water to wash his diapers.

CHAPTER SEVEN

JACK LEHR

Dad lost one eye due to a metal grinding accident. We knew him to wear a patch as he worked out of doors and a glass eye whenever he was in public.

Dad was a forward-thinking grain farmer. He was one of the first in the area to use the no-till approach, and as a result, he grew crops that far exceeded bushels per acre of other farmers in the area. He grew flax when others were growing wheat and oats. I remember the beautiful lavender flax crop as it came into bloom and rippled and waved in the wind.

While Dad was a successful grain farmer, we know that the farm could have consistently been a successful mixed farm. It seems that Dad tried to make this happen at one time. Don recalls when Dad came home from Regina with one hundred young pigs, and Don and Earl became pig farmers for a time. Sadly, Don remembers loading the pigs to take to Regina and Dad later returning with no cash from their sale. I'm sure there was much disappointment when the boys' work resulted in such a feeling of loss.

You see, Dad was a gambling poker player. As is often the case when a person has any addiction, loss and hurt and disappointment are the result for loved ones.

Mom didn't talk to us about Dad's gambling, but Aunty Mary told us that Mom was conflicted about it. When he came home with gambling money, she was happy to spend the money even though she didn't like his gambling.

Dad owned and operated a race car called #10. He raced in competition and was a very successful winner. The racing association soon created a new policy that would prevent him from competition. That policy effectively and intentionally prohibited anyone from competing who had suffered the loss of one eye, thereby effectively and purposely excluding him from competition. Dad hired a driver to race his car, but he was obviously not the driver that Dad was. He was soon knocked out of the competition.

Dad was a very smart and creative person. In 1952 and 1954, he created alternative systems to improve the functioning of vehicles. At the time he was associated with a couple of men in the area and I'm not sure why he assigned a percentage of his invention to these two men, but I suspect it was due to financial need.

John Lehr filed a CANADIAN PATENT #188034 on 18th of November1952 for VENTILATION SYSTEM FOR GAS TANKS and assigned to Floyd Fuder of Irma and David G Russell of Jarrow 20% to each of all his rights for a period of 17 years.

John Lehr filed a CANADIAN PATENT #485975 on the 19th day of August 1952 for CONE CAP FOR GAS TANKS AND THE LIKE and assigned to Floyd Fuder of Irma and David G. Russell of Jarrow 20% to each of all his rights for a period of 17 years.

John Lehr filed a UNITED STATES OF AMERICA PATENT #2,684,176 on July 20th, 1954 for CLOSURE FOR GAS TANKS AND THE LIKE and assigned to Floyd Fuder of Irma and David G Russell of Jarrow 20% to each of all his rights for a period of 17 years.

Race car #10. Dad was very successful in race car competitions in Regina, Saskatoon, and Moose Jaw. The boys were all called to work on the initial race car. Later a sponsor was able to fine-tune #10.

CHAPTER EIGHT

FUN AND GAMES

It seems that raising pigs was not all work and no play as Don told us how Earl used to ride them. They would first corral the pigs. Then, while Earl stood at the gate, Don chased the pigs through and Earl jumped on and went for a rough ride.

I don't think pigs buck and twist like a steer or a horse might, but the boys succeeded in making do with what was available. This would have been very funny, and I wish I had observed it myself.

We had other animals on the farm. Don had a dog that he called Ace. Ace was Don's best friend and one of the reasons Don never wanted to leave the farm.

And then there were the chickens that Mom raised. Eggs were a big part of our diet on the farm. And whenever our families from Moose Jaw came to visit, they expected a great chicken feast. I recall one time we came home from someplace where we had been, and Uncle Bill had already caught himself a chicken. We came home to a fully prepared roast chicken dinner.

Chickens grow through different stages of course from wee fuzzy little chicks, to gangly-legged middle-aged ones, and finally to the big rooster or the fluffy laying hens.

Russ and I were running around the yard one day chasing a funny-looking gangly-legged chick. As it headed into the garage, we just knew this would not go well with Dad, so we headed the chick toward the door. I was outside guarding, and just as the chick ran through the door, in my excitement, I trapped the chick in the door.

Well, this was not good. Russ, with his great four-year-old knowledge of the mechanics of fixing things, decided we needed to fix it by stuffing the insides back in. The chick wouldn't stay still so Russ suggested we put it in the vise to hold it still while we got the job done, so we did exactly how he had seen Dad do when he wanted to hold some inanimate piece of metal still. The idea was a good one, but unfortunately, it was a failure and the chick didn't recover. If I recall correctly, it was at that point that Mom appeared on the scene. Mom had an uncanny intuition and always seemed to be keeping an eye out to see what her children were up to when they were quiet or out of sight for a while.

As I heard this next story told by my family in later years, I felt embarrassed. Russ and I were good pals and we often played imaginary games — games that involved just the two of us. One sunny afternoon, as we were wandering around the yard marvelling at life and the world, we peeked into the brand-new chicken shed by the house. The hens were roosting; we decided to join them. They looked so content perched there silently on their roost. With a child's sense of reason, we knew that we could not just march in and change the whole scene, so we carefully removed our clothing and found our place on the chicken roost.

It was a solemn, peaceful wonder we experienced perching there in all our natural attire. I don't know how long we were there, probably not long, but that's how our mother found us. She quickly shooed us off the roosts and into the house to re-clothe ourselves. Now I think Mom handled this very delicately and she didn't scold or reprimand us, but I recall hearing the story come back to me in a teasing way and was embarrassed that others thought it was weird or funny.

The lucky chickens didn't mind. They got to sit and roost; after all, they didn't have clothes. Even today, Don chuckles when I tell this story.

CHAPTER NINE

IFIELD SCHOOL DAYS

The Ifield schoolyard was just a half-mile from our farmhouse. It had been closed when we first moved there and that's why we had been going to school at Golf School which was much farther away. Our new school was within walking distance. Ifield school was a one-room school that served grades one to eight.

Mom worked with the political system and the department of education to get this school opened. Some of the pluses were that it was still in fair condition and there was a teacherage in the same yard. One of the conditions was that the school had opened based on minimal enrolment. There were three of us Lehr kids, two Somerville kids, and Davey Miller. The next year, Russ had to start grade one when he was barely five to keep the enrolment up and growing and that continued as long as the school was open and as long as we lived in that area.

I was in grade one when the school opened. The first teacher I remember was Mr. Klassen, a middle-aged man who I thought was old. I remember that I didn't like him much. I don't know why, but I don't think he was very friendly. I think he was only there for a short term.

Miss Janiskavich was our next teacher, and as you can imagine, the thing I remember most about her was her name. It was lonely in that location for a single lady. I think she became friends with Mom and did visit our home sometimes on holidays. She taught at Ifield for one or two years.

Mrs. Lester was the next teacher. She had a little girl called Joy that started grade one with Roger. I didn't like it when they did spell drills and Joy was so smart and aced it every time while Roger was way further behind. It didn't bother him, but I took to trying to coach him at recess. He didn't like that so much and soon Mom asked me not to do that.

Mrs. Lester was a great teacher. We all liked her, and she became good friends with Mom. They were of like minds about teaching the whole child and she and Mom collaborated to make that happen.

We were introduced to various activities aside from our regular academics. I think she was quite firm and strict; I recall that she used a type of reward system. When we completed our required studies, we were involved in a lot of activities that today would be considered extracurricular.

We developed a strong school identity and participated in activities that allowed us to excel in the surrounding communities.

Our Christmas concerts were the best in the area and people came from far away. We practiced and memorized parts for plays that far exceeded the usual. Remember that there were only ten of us in attendance from five years to fourteen years, and these Christmas concerts were three hours long.

During this time, we learned to sing carols and dance the French minuet. We had a musical band that everyone participated in. I was proud to be selected as the conductor for the band.

Summertime activities were no less impressive as we participated in track and field days across the school division. We did relay racing, ball pitch, hundred-yard dash, and high jump as well as standing and running broad jump. We marched in the opening events and carried a school banner with our school name, IFIELD.

During the time that Mrs. Lester was taking us through the paces, Dad was digging pits for jumping, building high jump stands, and preparing the schoolyard for running tracks.

At the same time, Mom was busy at the sewing machine. She made costumes for Christmas concerts and uniforms for our track and field. We were ever so smart in our white shorts and shirts with shoulder banners displaying "Ifield" in black letters. We even had caps to match.

All the effort paid off in student, teacher, and parent pride for our accomplishments. We brought home a majority of first and second place ribbons after competing against much larger schools than ours. It still gives me a warm and proud feeling as I recall this time.

It was Mrs. Lester who started the hot lunch program during the winter as our family took turns bringing hot food to simmer on the kitchen stove in the teacherage.

At some time during Mrs. Lester's last year, grandkids of the neighbours started attending our school. These kids had been attending Regina schools and brought some bad attitudes with them. The boy came first; he was a bully over the young kids and tormented the girls. We didn't like him very much.

Our next teacher was Anne. I can't recall her last name. I think she may have been a new teacher and I believe she was quite overwhelmed by the task at hand. For the first time, the strap came into play. I still don't know what that was about, but I do remember that every one of us from grade one up experienced the corporal punishment. She was very angry, and I understood later it was because one of the older boys had started a rumour about her relationship with Leo, the gentleman farmer who lived across the fence from the schoolyard.

I still think that was very unfair, especially in light that she married that same gentleman at the year's end and they moved to a property across from ours.

Don admired Leo's large machinery and longed to be able to drive it. One day he was offered that opportunity and Don went to work for Leo and Anne Lynch. With the money he earned, he bought a bicycle.

When it was time for us to move from our farm, Don did not want to go. He wanted to take his dog Ace and live and work with Leo and Anne.

Mom was not ready to let her family be separated and she refused to allow him to go. Don and I recently pondered what staying behind would have meant for Don. I believe that Don would have become an important part of that family. I am thankful that my brother stayed with us though because I have enjoyed our senior years as the only surviving members of our family of origin.

There are so many other memories that flood our minds as we think back on life at the farm.

But at some point, I must conclude this record of those memories and move on the next chapters of our lives with a mother that we loved so dearly.

Proud Ifield school track team

CHAPTER TEN

Neighbours

We didn't often have guests over for dinner. There are a few times I remember when Uncle Bill Kergan was marketing aluminum cooking sets and he came and cooked a full-course dinner in his new shiny pots and pans as he demonstrated to several of our neighbours the value of cooking with little water to preserve the flavour and nutrients. I don't know how much he sold, but a complete set of these heavy aluminum pots, including the roaster, were in our home long after aluminum pots were declared unsafe.

Our neighbours down the road were the young Abby Bechard family. I was fascinated with babies, and so one day, feeling the need for more neighbourly social interaction, I begged Mom to let me invite the Bechard family for a last-minute Sunday dinner. Last minute it was, and I was given permission to ride to the neighbours and invite them without the expectation that they would accept. Well, they did. When I got back home, I discovered that the family dinner had begun without me and my guests. I think there was some fancy scurrying about as the new dinner guests joined us for a leftover Sunday dinner.

A young neighbour friend, Ellen Sommerville, shared many adult stories with me, including telling me about male predators and how they behaved. It was also Ellen who first told me about adoption, something I had no knowledge of. She explained to me that Earl was not really my brother but that he was adopted and that was why he was very different from the rest of us. I was stunned and told her she didn't know what she was talking about. I was so sure she was wrong that I jokingly told Earl what she had said. His reaction was immediate anger.

His words were, "So that's why!" I felt very responsible for hurting him in that way.

I have always wished I had talked to Mom, for she may have been able to explain it to him. Mom said she had tried to tell him many times when he was younger, but she really didn't think of him as anything other than her true son. I guess she never thought about the fact that other people talk. As I have said, children listen to adult conversations and often relay that information inappropriately.

The area where we lived in Saskatchewan must have been one of the places in the world where trees are very scarce. One year the agricultural powers that be decided to give away trees to farmers to plant as shelterbelts. Dad came home with a truckload and gathered the family together to begin planting.

We did, all five-strong of us, measuring to be sure they were nicely spaced and into the ground. Could have been a nice shelter belt and would surely have been beautiful. Unfortunately, the trees did not thrive in the soil without adequate water. As fortune would have it, the neighbour, Abby Bechard, dug a trench on his property, threw the trees in, and covered them up. They survived. I'm not sure what the lesson is; maybe that's what people call Karma.

CHAPTER ELEVEN

WHERE LOVE RESIDES

One lazy afternoon at school I was excitedly telling my friend Ellen Somerville about my summer plan to visit Grandma. I talked about the fact that Mom had said she would get me a new swimsuit that year and I was so looking forward to getting it so that I could go swimming with Aunty Mary and Grandma.

I was crushed when Ellen uttered in the most sarcastic tone, "No wonder your family is poor." I hadn't thought of myself as poor, but that's how I found out we were considered poor by our neighbours.

Ours was not a family of wealth, but we were not poor. We did not have a fancy home, but we did not want for anything. We were raised in a loving family. We participated fully in community events including fowl suppers, sports and field days, bridal showers, berry-picking excursions, church vacation school, visits to Grandma Cross, and neighbourhood indoor board game competitions.

Mom was an amazing cook and we always had substantial meals as we ate together as a family around our oak dining table. We were never allowed to leave the table without requesting to be excused. We did our homework at this same oak table that carried the scars of pencils and scratches.

For our lunch we brought healthy sardine sandwiches, canned chicken dinners, and bread pudding dessert with raisins.

Favourite foods I recall are bread pudding with raisins and home-made bread fresh from the oven. I recall watching to see if Mom would bake her famous bread product that she made especially for Dad. She called it German buns because Grandma Lehr had shown her how to make these flattened crusty buns baked with a liberal brushing of butter.

There was a swing in the yard just across from the garden where I took my dolls and played house all by myself.

My dolls were a real family, and they were great company for me. As a young child, I think I often felt the solitude and loneliness of being "the girl." I would swing and play there for long periods of time by myself. I played with dolls until I was really a bit too old for that, but they were not just dolls; they were a real family to me.

My favourite books were always about families: *Heidi* and *Five Little Peppers* were two favourites. I also read the boys' books: *Black Beauty*, *Tom Sawyer*, *Huckleberry Finn*, and *The Hardy Boys*. Mom's Aunt Edie used to send a bundle of books at Christmas time. They were always classic books that stood the test of time. Don and I are still avid readers today, a tribute to a mother whom we saw read everything in sight. We saw her read *Gone with The Wind* over and over when reading materials were scarce.

From a very young age, I knew that it was a family expectation that I would become a registered nurse. Grandma promised me a nurse's watch to pin on my uniform when I graduated. I didn't become a registered nurse, but I often played the part of a nurse or a teacher when I could con one of my brothers into playing house with me. I think that my intrigue with families influenced my early desire to be married and have a large family.

When Mom figured it was time for me to learn what being a girl really meant, she came one night and snuggled with me in my bed and told me the story of how life begins. I wish I could remember exactly what she told me because it was very beautiful. It made me happy to be a girl who was ready to become a woman. It's just one of those times with Mom I treasure.

I know that Mom had conversations with the boys which paralleled this teaching where she instilled in them the virtues of being men of high standards.

CHAPTER TWELVE

Always a Mom, Always a Teacher

Mom was great at teaching by example. Today I think they call it interactive learning or something special like that. When the carpenters came to work on Ifield school, we were the closest neighbours. Mom was asked to provide meals for the work crew. Mom enlisted me to help and I was more than excited to take on this new big girl role. I remember helping to prepare the food and setting the table just right. I remember the apron I wore and the way I learned to serve the workers from their left side. I learned that was the correct way to serve so that you weren't passing the food in front of the diner.

I recall we were always ready for the work crew when they arrived and received great praise for what we provided. It was such a good experience and taught me more than I thought at the time. Mom was paid for this service and she shared the profits with me.

People have asked why Mom didn't teach our illiterate Dad to read and write. I am not sure when, but she did teach him to write his own name, a skill that he hadn't learned until they met. I'm guessing he didn't want to sign his marriage certificate with an X as he would have done before. I think that the busyness of farm and family may have been the reason why she didn't continue her lessons, or perhaps it was just more difficult for an adult learner at that time than as it is now.

Dad was very proud of Mom's education and he encouraged her when it became necessary for her to apply some political pressure to have Ifield school opened and maintained for several years. I recall him teasing her about her support for the politician Tommy Douglas and I also recall hearing him encourage her with, "You go, Dione, you go!"

SECTION TWO

CHAPTER THIRTEEN

THE FAMILY IN CRISIS

Late in the fall of 1948, Dad was advised that the farm had been sold and his rental agreement was over. I think that it is fair to say that Dad was in shock. I am being very generous in looking back at these events and trying to understand that this was perhaps the beginning of a depression that altered Dad's emotional life. He would never recover.

Dione was not a naive wife. There were many signs that all was not well in the marriage, but I think it's safe to say that she was caught unawares one evening when Jack arrived home to announce that he was having an affair and he was leaving the marriage and family.

Don reported having overheard this conversation and Mom replying angrily, "So just how am I expected to feed our children?"

And with that, our family would move into the next phase of our lives as Dione straightened up and began to plan to return to teaching and raising her family as a single parent. Mom never shared her pain with me or any of her children.

It was a bitterly cold morning in the small Saskatchewan town of Sedley when a lady in her late thirties walked into the train station and bought an adult one-way ticket to Regina, Saskatchewan. She also bought tickets for her five children. A neighbour friend, Art Somerville, stood on the wooden platform and watched as she turned from the ticket wicket. Aware of the station master's curious stares, she gathered her children and their luggage and moved outdoors. We stood waiting for the train that would take us on the first leg of the journey into the future.

She was a pretty lady, her face saddened with worry and an unspoken fear. Neighbour Art strode over to her, offered his hand, and said something softly to her. She gave him an embarrassed smile as she thanked him for his assistance in bringing her to this spot.

The lady was warmly dressed in a brown mutton fur coat and headscarf; she was used to the cold winters. She carried a rather large purse and a handknit shopping bag. Her children stayed close, not fully understanding the significance of the Moment.

While we stood waiting for the train to thunder to a stop, us children, aged two to fourteen years, tugged at the luggage. There were six pieces of luggage: a two-piece set of blue leather with tan binding, a dark blue tin trunk, and some boxes tied with string. The friendly, uniformed conductor placed the little stool on the platform and greeted each of us, offering a good day and a hand to help us up the train steps. He directed us through the coach to our seats and stowed the luggage overhead.

It was not the first train ride for us and we scurried along through the coach, seemingly unaware of the dire situation we were embarking upon. *I have no choice,* she told herself as she gathered the baby onto her lap and silently said a prayer of thanks for her mother who had insisted that she complete her teacher training at a normal school in Moose Jaw at age eighteen. It had been such a happy time, but it all seemed so long ago. She was tired.

The train slowly moved out from the station and Dione closed her eyes and leaned back against the headrest. She mourned for the family life she had dreamed of. She thought of Earl, the eldest son she had to leave behind in Regina to finish his grade nine. Earl had been boarding in Regina and would finish out the school year there with a young RCMP family in exchange for babysitting their young daughter in the evenings when they attended events.

A rush of thoughts flashed through her mind as the past few months came into focus. Was it only such a short time ago that she and Jack had discussed the beginning of the end of their future together? She'd known for some time that they couldn't carry on the way they were. They had children to think of, six of them. It was in September when he told her the quarter section they farmed and lived on had been sold.

She refused to concern herself with the many reasons for the marriage problems; it was too painful. She had agreed that she would return to teaching because although Jack talked big plans to buy some heavy equipment and find jobs to support them, in her heart Dione knew that she couldn't rely on him to take care of them. She was embarrassed that the neighbours and her family knew that Jack was cheating on her and that he was gambling excessively and drinking. She did her best to shield the children from these realities but somehow, we sensed the tension. The absence of our father for days at a time was really a dead giveaway. I was just nine when I first understood the quarrelling late into the night in the bedroom next to mine. The boys, Don and Russ, had been with our dad on some of his excursions to Regina and had witnessed the betrayal firsthand.

Her thoughts wandered back to the state things had been left in at the home on the farm. Everything was packed and stacked. The movers had been contacted, but they couldn't get through until after the New Year due to the severe weather conditions. Dione was not sure she would ever see any of our possessions again.

My recollection of leaving the farm is sketchy. Dad was conspicuously absent during the period before the sale, and he was not present at the sale of the family home or during the pack-up time at all. Earl was taking his grade nine in Regina, so it was Don, Russ, and Mom that prepared the small amount of machinery and tools to be auctioned when the sale occurred on a blustering freezing day in December. Machinery auctioned including tractors, combine, swather, and all the shop tools. The sale of the Allis Chalmers tractor was stopped because the auctioneer was not satisfied with the bids that were forthcoming.

Everything else was sold at give-away prices. Although I can't remember how many dollars were recovered, Don says he think it was nine hundred dollars. I do remember that the auctioneer was very disappointed for her. He knew the family situation and he advised her to make sure that she held on to the money for herself and her children. I don't recall ever hearing Mom speak of the farm or the sale again. Mom was a master at keeping her pain to herself and protecting her children from the harsh truth of life. My siblings and I understood that Mom was hurt, and we chose not to speak about anything that hurt her.

When the train pulled into Regina, the family scurried through the huge train station with its shiny, hard marble floors, huge oak and brass doors, and long oak benches. Stopping only briefly while Mom bought the next set of tickets, we boarded the train for the next leg of our journey to Saskatoon. We disembarked and re-boarded in Saskatoon, and when we re-boarded, Dad joined us for the rest of our trip to Chauvin, Alberta. I don't recall questioning this. Perhaps because he had already begun drifting in and out of our lives a couple of years before, we were conditioned to it.

Don tells me when they met at the train station, Mom counted out one half of the auction money and told him he could have the tractor. Some years later, Aunty Mary told us that Grandma Cross was very upset with Mom for doing that. Mom responded, "He is my husband; he's entitled to his half."

I understand this as an act of defiance expressing her anger: *If he doesn't want me, then I don't want anything from him.* Oddly enough, I believe I would do the same.

The next part of the trip took us through the night. It took a lot longer to travel by train in 1949 than it does now in 2019. We stretched out on the double seats that were turned to face each other and covered ourselves with our coats. I don't recall what we ate. I think that Mom had food in the large shopping bag she carried. I do know there were washrooms and a drinking fountain on one of the other coaches and we had to cross a bridge between the coaches to get to it.

CHAPTER FOURTEEN

ARRIVING IN CHAUVIN

As we stood on the railway platform at Chauvin, Dad stayed on the train and travelled on to Edmonton. I couldn't help but wonder what Mom was thinking and feeling. I think of the phrase we have used since to describe a brave act: With head up and shoulder to the load, she strode forth to the only place to stay.

I think those first days in a new town were exciting for us kids. Yet we knew then, and I know today, the terrific stress that this was for our mother.

We arrived with only the clothing we could pack in the old suitcases and boxes. The furniture was left on the farm in Saskatchewan to be picked up by a moving van when they could get through the winter storms.

After leaving the train station in Chauvin, we went directly to the hotel where Mom booked us a couple of rooms. I am not sure what kind of arrangements she had made with the hotel owner, but I know she didn't have money. She had only the promise of a job at the local school.

Somehow, we managed to eat and had a warm place to sleep for the few days until school started. I don't remember how, but Mom scouted us out a house to live in when our furniture arrived. The house, a two-storey in decent condition, was owned by Mr. Shantz, a local mechanic.

I can't imagine how Mom managed the rental arrangement because she had no money. People were different in those days. When the furniture arrived, Mom had no money to pay the mover. I do remember the silent sense of dread we all felt as the movers threatened to return our furniture. Fortunately, Mom negotiated with the mover to pay him later.

The first task in our new home was to put up the window covers, adapting them as needed. Then it was time to unpack the bedding and make the beds. The rest of the unpacking could get done as time and need occurred.

Classrooms were three grades to a class and Mom got busy preparing for her primary grade classes. Mom used a duplicator to prepare lessons. Sitting at a small table in the hotel room, she handwrote all the student work using an indelible pen. The duplicator was a large cookie sheet filled with a duplicating gel that had to be heated and poured into the tray. Then she laid the handwritten page she had prepared and smoothed it to the gel. She then was able to duplicate by placing a fresh sheet of paper on the gel, pressing it down, and then pulling up carefully so as not to blur the ink. She was able to make several copies from one set of gel and then she would melt that down and start over.

Don was in grade eight and I was in grade seven. Our classroom teacher was Mrs. Cargill. By the time we all got settled at the school, Mom had located a babysitter for Gordie who was just past two at that time. Mom was such a strong and proud lady who humbled herself over and over for us as our family grew over the years. We were so blessed to have her for our Mom.

The position in Chauvin was temporary, so after attending summer school in Edmonton to upgrade her teaching certificate, Mom made the decision to take a teaching position at the Holt Hutterite Colony by Irma.

We had to pack again. China cabinet contents of crystal and special china were wrapped carefully and packed while the china cabinet was wrapped at the last minute in quilts to protect the glass door. Pictures would have been removed from the walls and carefully packed in boxes or trunks.

Lastly, bedding was folded, beds dismantled, and the window coverings were removed and packed.

Dad moved to Irma at this time. He would be with us at times and then he would leave for a time.

These were my parents' strange living arrangements. Mom didn't discuss adult things with us, and we never expected Dad to stay long. If we did comment, we were told "He is still my husband and he's your father."

As I write about this, I think it was a very strange way for a couple to live. I really don't understand what Mom thought about this arrangement, but I don't recall asking about it. Maybe we thought that they would work out their differences, whatever they were. It is more likely that perhaps we were so used to not understanding adult ways that we simply accepted it.

CHAPTER FIFTEEN

HOME AT THE HUTTERITE COLONY

At the Holt Colony, Mom basically taught in a one-room school with grades one to eight. This would be quite a switch from teaching in Chauvin. In addition, Mom was now teaching her family in a public school system. Gordie, who was still too young to start school, spent days at the Hutterite colony nursery school.

One attraction of this teaching appointment was that there was a large old three-bedroom ranch house that would serve as our family home for two years. It was a very old house at the top of a hill with a temperamental generating system. It was here that twelve-year-old Russ began to demonstrate his creative mechanical ability. Many times, Russ was challenged with tinkering and coaxing this generator back to life to provide us with light to start and end the day for the many rooms of this home. The home had a primitive type of forced air furnace, and with the help of our mechanically creative brother, we were nearly always warm and cozy. A temperamental and shallow well provided water for most of the family's daily needs. The home had no indoor plumbing, but an old outhouse accommodated our personal sanitary needs. I recall there was a large open kitchen/dining area with a wood stove and a lot of built-in cupboards; a huge living room with a fireplace; and, surrounding that, one wall was built in library type shelving. The floors, as I recall, were hardwood.

Our arrival at our new home included a ritual that was to be revisited several times over the next years.

Window covers were shaken out and installed on all windows. Next came the chore of setting up the beds and making them all up so they would be ready to crawl into as soon as they were needed.

The first challenge that Mom faced was that the Hutterite colony had just located there, and a schoolhouse had not yet been built. Mom offered the use of our living room as a classroom, and that's where she began teaching. I believe it may have been three months into the school term before the new schoolhouse was ready for occupancy. Mom was to teach three members of our family in that one-room school: me in grade eight, Russ in grade seven, and Roger in grade four.

I regret to say we were not the easiest students to teach. Russ and I often didn't attend classes. Instead, we slept late and hung around the house. While I'm sure our absence caused Mom stress, I don't think she had the energy to deal with it. For us, it meant we were that much further behind in our studies. The result of this would follow us through to our next classroom.

Other challenges for the family had to do with high school education for Earl, who returned to the family group in grade eleven; and for Don, in grade ten. Wainwright school division accommodated high school students by providing a boarding home style of living in Wainwright for a limited number of high school students. Earl and Don lived there in a dormitory residence for two years. I joined them in the second year to begin grade nine. As I recall, the cost of attending this boarding school was $45.00 a month. That meant that our high school education was costing Mom $135 a month from her salary. I don't recall her ever discussing these fees with us and the hardship that it cost her, but I do know that I personally did not appreciate this opportunity.

Earl and I continued to live in the dormitory and attend school in Wainwright until Earl graduated from grade twelve and I completed grade nine. Don had decided that school was not for him and he ventured forth into the work world where he worked for a local farmer north of Jarrow. It was during this time that Don developed an interest in community dances and walked a half-mile to meet up with the Oracheskis to practice the dance lessons he had learned years earlier during his attendance at Ifield school. Don recalls accompanying Eli Tschetter to sell chickens. According to the story, every time Eli sold a chicken, they would go to the bar and get beer, and they would end up at the dance hall in Kinsella.

At Easter, when all the adults were attending church, several of my Hutterite friends decided to see what I would look like as a Hutterite and proceeded to help clothe me in the traditional dress. They even parted my hair in the middle and rolled it back under a polka dot kerchief. Paul, one of the Huttterite boys, showed a definite interest in me. Soon after this, Mom decided that I really needed to leave and go away to school lest our romance developed into something serious.

With all the challenges Mom faced in getting to this point in her life journey, I believe that she was somewhat content and felt protected and safe here for a couple of years.

We were considered a part of a caring community who tended to some of our needs such as delivering food to us on a Saturday evening (freshly baked buns, eggs, chickens, and delicious chicken noodle soup). Sometimes this was delivered by one or two of the young men along with guitars and a desire to sing and visit. We were invited to use the communal laundry and communal bathing area. We accessed these on a limited basis because we were taught to respect the offers with temperance.

On Sunday evenings, it was necessary for us to get to Irma to board the train to Wainwright. Often, one or more of the young Hutterite men were more than willing to take a quick trip into Irma and we were able to get rides there and back to school in Wainwright in this somewhat haphazard way.

Although Jack Lehr essentially abandoned his wife and family when we got on the train at Regina, that did not mean he was out of our lives. I guess from afar we can try to understand what went on between Mom and Dad, and we could lay blame and cast doubts about many things. I know that although Mom was heartbroken over her marriage, she never shared with us any of her grief except for one time telling me to stay close to her and never consider going to live with my dad. I didn't question her request because I had no intention of going anywhere. She never downgraded our father's character. That's strength and that's character and that's integrity. That's also darn tough to maintain. When Dione married Jack Lehr in 1929, she made a vow before God to stay true to her marriage. Dione Lehr would keep that vow of "in sickness and in health, for richer and poorer." There was no room for us to question Mom's attitude about this, and even in private we never did.

One spring at the Hutterite colony, an explosion occurred in the kitchen range that resulted in severe burn injuries to Mom and five-year-old Gordie. Gordie was wearing a parka with a wolf fur-trimmed hood. This caught fire and caused burns and thick scarring that Gordie carried throughout his life. Mom was also burned. They were hospitalized in Viking, Alberta.

The doctors stated that Gordie only survived because Mom would not have him taken from her arms throughout the days and nights after. I recall my first visit to the hospital. Gordie's entire head and upper body were encased in a huge cast-like bandage. It was very difficult to see my mom and baby brother in that condition.

We were able to care for ourselves during Mom's absence. Mom was discharged from the hospital first and Gordie stayed for about a week longer. When Mom was leaving the hospital, she made arrangements that I should work in the hospital cleaning wards for the time that Gordie was there. My task was to ensure that Dad didn't take him. I later learned that Dad had threatened her that he would take Gordie. This was only one of the empty threats we came to expect from him. This sounds rather bizarre to me as I write it, and I can't explain how that could have been, but that's what happened.

CHAPTER SIXTEEN

TEACHING ASSIGNMENT AT SYDENHAM SCHOOL

The only reason I can think of for Mom accepting this teaching assignment at Sydenham school is that she had run out of choices. She had been attending summer schools to upgrade her teaching certificate and was receiving good reports for her teaching performance from the superintendent of schools, but she also had an estranged husband who was constantly causing issues in the community. I believe this was having a negative impact on her reputation and was perceived as reflective on the community school. We were not aware of this at the time.

Dione and the family had challenges prior to the placement at Sydenham but the worst was yet to come.

The school was a one-room rural classroom located about four miles north of Wainwright. Living arrangements would plague her. The family was going through transitions. Earl was graduating, Don had left school, and me, Russ, Roger, and Gordie were still in school.

A little old farmhouse was located and at some point, there was a vehicle in our possession. (I believe Earl was the driver, though I'm not sure where this vehicle came from.) For the first months of school, we lived here at the Nichol house and attended school in Wainwright, dropping Mom and Gordie off at Sydenham.

Then, for whatever reason, we relocated to the two-storey Woodward house and continued to live there for the winter.

Transportation soon became an issue again. Mom moved into the basement of the school and rented a little old house in Wainwright where the boys and I lived. This allowed Mom to meet her obligation to the school, but I recall this as the worst time in my childhood. Earl was intolerable and demanding, and he had expectations beyond what could be met. Even though I was much too young and inexperienced to manage a household and still attend school, that is what was expected of me for approximately four months. Russ didn't want to go to school and often didn't. Roger was suffering emotional neglect in this situation and was doing poorly, so Mom took him to live with her at Sydenham.

It was during this traumatic time that I began dating a young man named Charlie Wakefield who would one day become my husband. I had met Charlie while we were in the dormitory and attending school. While attending a community dance with my brothers, he asked me for a date.

The living arrangements and being separated from Mom was not working for our family. Mom was able to negotiate with the school board at Sydenham to relocate us all to the basement of the school. What a strange experience that must have seemed to anyone else in the neighbourhood. We rode bicycles to high school in Wainwright.

Charles Wakefield, my boyfriend, transported groceries to us and often served as transportation as we needed it. He was an amazing young man. Later, in April 1953, we would marry. I was sixteen years old.

Life, while not ideal, became more comfortable because we were together as a family again and Mom was there to make us feel safe and whole again.

While we spent the summer in this far from ideal living arrangement, Mom had us all under one roof. I recall that summer as a relatively happy one. Mom seemed more content. Grandma and our aunts and uncles visited us that summer. We hadn't seen them for some time. Aunt Mary, Mom's sister, stayed to spend time with us. Mom loved her sister and had a strong bond with her.

Another move was on the horizon though and this time it was a positive choice. We would move to Edgerton where Mom would teach grade five & six. I recall Aunty Mary saying it was perfect because they had an active Anglican church there.

St. Mary's Anglican Church in Edgerton was to play a hugely important role in Mom's future. Mom finally had opportunity to practice her faith in earnest. During this time, our family life began to take on a positive sense of normalcy.

CHAPTER SEVENTEEN

LIFE IN EDGERTON, ALBERTA

Edgerton, being a village, had housing available, but the clincher was that there was an active Anglican church in town. Aunty Mary and Mom's excitement was a source of joy around our home while Mom made the arrangements to make this move before school started. It was the first time in a long time I could remember her being happy and excited. Dione accepted a position at Edgerton teaching grades five and six in September 1952. For the first time, we began hearing Mom referred to by her first name, Edith. On reflection I assume this was in reference to the name on her teaching certificate.

Although Mom had prearranged to rent a home for her family in Edgerton, there were some complications with the previous renter's lease and there was no accommodation available for a few months.

So, Mom negotiated with Bob and Mary Harkness to allow us to live in a somewhat unorthodox way for those months. Mom rented a room in the Edgerton Tavern and she and Gordie resided there while the rest of our family had accommodation in a storage shed at the back of the lot.

We were able to cook and sleep there. The Harkness family were very helpful during this time of settlement and we washed our clothing in the laundry room of the tavern. It was here where we began our exposure to the Edgerton community.

During this time of getting settled in Edgerton, Dad's younger brother, Uncle Harry, and his wife, Aunt Louise, became involved in our family's life.

Our family was very fond of Uncle Harry and Aunt Louise. We appreciated their involvement as they visited faithfully every spring and fall for many years.

Eventually, we were able to settle into our home next door to the Anglican church. Four of us were enrolled in the Edgerton school: me, Russ, Roger, and Gordie. Mom began teaching.

One of Mom's former students from this class, Carole Kimball, later married my brother Don. She tells of her fond memories of Mrs. Lehr, her grade five teacher, who later she called Mom Lehr. Carole also recalls that Roger was a challenge for Mom in class and she tells of one time that Mom had to say, "Roger, you sit down right now!" in a sterner voice than she used with her other students. The following year, in September, Mom was given the opportunity to teach grade one. Now she was happy; she loved this grade one class. Her former students tell me that they loved her. This make me happy.

Russ travelled the road with a friend, Doug Hicox, for a period of time. They were known to travel in an old beater with a loaf of bread and a hunk of bologna. Doug told the story of how he and Russ decided one morning that they would join the Navy. While walking to the recruiting office, a young lady caught Russ's eye, and as he turned to keep her in his sight line, he walked straight into a street lamp knocking himself out cold. They didn't make it to the recruiting office and so the Navy would miss out on a couple of fine recruits.

Mom had a belief in encouraging the development of young people through community involvement.

Mom, as guide captain, started the first Edgerton Guide company with twenty-five guides and was assisted by Miss Jean Kett and Miss Francis Foley as lieutenants.

Mom was a warranted guider. She took the guides on the first of several unofficial guide camps where they enjoyed swimming, hiking, handicraft, learning to cook over a campfire, and so many things about woodlore and nature. She was accompanied to this camp by her sister, Mary Kergan, who had travelled from Moose Jaw to be acting assistant. Years later, Roger's wife, Myrna, would also serve the Edgerton Guide company as a qualified lifeguard and swimming instructor. I remember being proud to attend the Mother-Daughter banquet held on Feb 22nd, observing Thinking Day, and celebrating the birthday of founders

Lord and Lady Baden-Powel. Years later, recalling the importance of Baden-Powell to the youth, I became a Cub Scout Leader.

For the first time in many years, Dione was able to enjoy pleasant companionship with several of her teaching colleagues. Margaret Bedford was one of those people. Margaret recalls the relationship they had with one such comment recorded in *WINDS OF CHANGE*, a community history book dedicated to the memory of our pioneers and compiled by the Edgerton Historical Society:

"Edith was teaching grade one at the time and Margaret was teaching grades 2 & 3. It was the school Christmas party and all the students had brought their younger brothers and sisters. It was just a few minutes before the one o'clock bell was to ring when the fire alarm went off. Edith and Margaret were in the hall wondering how they were ever going to get their students and guests out when Mr. Duke came rushing in with a funny look.

Immediately, Margaret and Edith looked at each other, wondering if one of their sons Roger or Doug had been mischief makers again. Turns out they were both involved. The story is that they were fooling around in the gym and accidentally knocked into the fire alarm. Or so the story goes." (p83)

The house at Edgerton still stands. If one were to look closely today, you might even see how the house suffered from Roger's baseball pitching practice and his hockey puck shots as he hammered the nearest south wall hour after hour. Sunday dinner would often be accompanied by the music of the baseball or the hockey puck repeatedly thumping against the south wall of the house.

This habit of Roger's proved to be of some value to him as he left to go to school in Wilcox College in Saskatchewan, with the intent of a hockey career. In January1958, Roger moved to Hardisty from Edgerton to join the Hardisty Stampeders hockey team. He was just sixteen years old at the time, soon to be seventeen with a January birthday. Mom gave her OK and signed his hockey contract with a request that Roger be encouraged to attend school while playing hockey.

The Lou and Charlotte Golka home became his residence and home for some time. He worked on the construction of the new Alberta Government Telephone building for a short time and then went to work at Hardisty Motors for Lou Golka, in sales. He did not return to school.

In early fall of 1959, The Edmonton Oil Kings drafted Roger. This required a move to Edmonton. He was doing well until November 25th of that year when he broke his ankle. The Oil Kings brought Roger back to play before his ankle was one hundred per cent healed and unfortunately, he reinjured the ankle.

In the fall of 1960 Roger returned to the Oil Kings with an early move to the Prince Albert Minto's. This was followed by a trade later that fall to the Estevan Bruins of the Saskatchewan Junior Hockey League for goalie Paul Sexsmith, who was considered the top Junior "A" goalie in western Canada at that time. Roger was pleased that he was traded for this calibre of player like Paul.

With this move, Roger became the property of the Boston Bruins organization. He would play with Estevan until Christmas break. At this time, he was not happy with the extreme travel schedule. He made a personal decision to return to Hardisty to play at the local level with the Hardisty Stampeders, and he went to work for Hardisty Motors.

Mom and all our family were very proud of our little brother's hockey achievements, but the proudest of all was his little brother Gordie. Gordie followed closely in Roger's footsteps.

Gordie was very involved in various sports teams in Edgerton. He played hockey and basketball; his real passion was baseball. He carried on the tradition of throwing the baseball against the house for hours on end. He loved to play catch with his big brother and took every opportunity to do this.

Mom was a member of St. Mary's Anglican church, a member of the church vestry, and a Sunday school teacher. Mom had ensured that all her children were baptised as infants and did her best to ensure that we remained faithful. She was instrumental in Charles' adult baptism and confirmation.

Teacher Jeanette Murray was a close friend and neighbour to Dione and her family. Jeanette was honoured to be asked by Russ to be Godmother to his daughter Debra.

An honour Mom received while teaching grade one was her work with Superintendent of schools Mr. Lindstead, as he based his Ph.D. thesis on Mom's work in developing a remedial reading program.

One day in 1961 Mom received a call from Dad's brother, Herb Lehr, in California. Herb informed her that Dad had apparently returned to his family. He had been in Los Angeles, California for a period of time and had collapsed on the street. He was taken to hospital and surgery was performed for a large brain tumor.

Earl and I went with Mom to see what his condition was. He was not doing that well, but he appeared to be recovering. Dad's brothers who lived in Los Angeles informed Mom that they were not prepared to care for him long-term. It seemed Dad would be homeless if he stayed there. Without hesitation, Mom decided to bring him home.

Remember that she had promised all those years ago that she would love him in sickness and in health? She was not about to abandon him now.

We stayed with Dad's brother's family while there, and then Earl and I returned home by car. About two weeks later, when Dad was well enough to travel, Mom brought him home to Edgerton by train.

Unfortunately, because of the invasive nature of his brain surgery, Dad quickly began to demonstrate serious personality disturbances that required Mom to have him committed to Ponoka Alberta hospital. Mom visited him there and found it very disturbing. Dad passed away on July 19 and was buried in Edgerton Cemetery.

Saint Mary's Anglican Church Edgerton 1927.

Edgerton collage. mom Gordie &roger. Moms church, mom and one of grandbabies

August 19th, 1962
Ponoka, Alberta.

Dear Paris:

This is just a brief line because I want to get it mailed right away. I got your letter when I got here on Saturday. Del drove me down and she and the children stayed overnight and went back this afternoon. About your holiday. I'm so glad you and Charles are planning a little jaunt on your own. Is there any way you can manage it so you can leave the children here with me, or any way part of them? You do have relatives who would enjoy having them you know. Carole & Don would enjoy keeping one or two or Del said she'd be glad to keep more than the baby. Although I know you are probably thinking that Baby is enough. Del is looking forward to having her. But Landor isn't here so I have plenty of room. If you want to leave the others here it would be fine. I haven't had a word from them for a long time. I was slow suggesting this wasn't I. Guess I just wasn't thinking very hard about family affairs. I think the exam might be O.K. it wasn't as hard as I had expected.

Well whatever you do have a good holiday —

love,
Mom.

This is the last letter I received from Mom.

Epilogue

Grandchildren Richard and Greg remember Grandma's place. They remember the tea they drank from real tea cups. They remember what it felt like to receive her loving hugs. Grandma Lehr cared for the grandchildren overnight many times and she watched over Earl's children as Earl and Del took a time out from family stress. Barbara has a faint memory of going on the train with Grandma Lehr on a trip to Moose Jaw where Grandma showed her off with great pride.

More than one wedding meal took place around Mom's table.

Sundays and holidays would always find several family members at Mom's house in Edgerton. She always had a full meal prepared and still insisted that we sit down together to a table set with a linen cloth and special dishes. Mom expected her grandchildren to comply with good table manners.

We followed this practice in our own family.

In 1962, all my siblings except for Gordie were married and raising our own families.

Charles had sought employment at DND Wainwright in Stores, later transferring to the DND electrical shop where he attained his journeyman electrician and refrigeration certification. I kept the home fires burning as a stay-at-home mom.

After Earl completed his graduation at Wainwright High, he took employment as an electrician apprentice at Iverson's Electric and later accepted a position as electrical foreman at the DND base in Wainwright. Later, he transferred to Yellowknife and went to work with Electrical Union Station taking a job in Fort MacMurray.

Don took employment with some local Irma farmers, Cecil Lockhart and George Theroux. He obtained employment at the Army base for Nu-West Construction, then for Eskimo Well Servicing where he perfected his skill at operating a cat.

Russ found employment with Nickel's garage at Edgerton and later Whalen Construction. He and his buddy Doug Hicox travelled around together for quite a period roughing it and working at the shipyards in BC where he learned the welding trade. Russ later worked on the construction of Gardner Dam in Saskatchewan.

By August 1962, Dione's family had increased severalfold.

Doris and husband Charles Wakefield and grandchildren Richard, Greg, Larry, Barbara, and Beverly.

Earl and wife Delores (Fayant) and grandchildren Sharon, Edith, Martha, and Herb.

Russ and wife Doreen (Kobasiuk) and daughter Debra were expecting Sheri.

Don and wife Carole (Kimball) were expecting Kevin.

Roger and wife Myrna (Oliver) were expecting Connie.

Gordie was sixteen years old and preparing to finish high school in Ponoka, Alberta.

In 1962, Dione graduated with a much-coveted Bachelor of Education from the University of Alberta. She made plans to move to a new position in Ponoka where she would teach History, a subject she loved.

Charles and I visited Mom in her new apartment on our way to a holiday in Banff. She went to the liquor store and insisted we drink wine to celebrate her well-earned degree.

She was very happy and looking forward to beginning this new stage of her life along with Gordie.

We talked about family during that time. We noted that Mom was so happy about how our family had pulled together and loved and cared for one another.

As we expressed our concern for Earl's mental health and well-being, Mom, in her usual concern for Earl, indicated she understood that Earl's mental health may be because of his feelings over his adoption. Shortly after this conversation, Earl returned home from fort MacMurray and Del reached out to Mom for help in response to Earl's strange behaviour that frightened her. Mom got on a bus in Ponoka and went to Earls home.

Little did we know that a heavy cloud was about to appear over all our lives.

TRAGEDY

While camping at Banff, Charlie got sick and so we drove into Calgary and took a hotel room. On the morning of August 30th, Charlie tuned the car radio to an Edmonton station, and we heard the following broadcast:

'Two Edmonton women murdered by a 26-year-old husband and son of the mother who adopted him."

Initially no names were announced but I immediately screamed in awareness that this was my family. I continued to scream as Charlie drove as fast as he could to Edmonton, all the while trying to console me with the thought that we really didn't know anything.

Before we reached my brother Don's home, the news announced their names. I only remember sobbing as Don met us at the door of his home with our baby daughter Beverly. They gave us as many details as they could.

Earl had returned home from Fort MacMurray and Mom had been called to come and see if she could calm him or get Earl to go to the hospital. Earl's wife Delores had arranged for the rest of the children to be taken to relatives in the city but chose to keep Beverly with her since it seemed that Earl was calmed by her presence.

I only know the details that follow from what others have told me. Uncle Bill picked up Mom and dropped her off at Earl's home. I was told the conversation at that time was that Uncle Bill would be back to check on her in a couple of hours and that Mom was confident that everything was okay.

All the family that lived in Edmonton including brother Russ were aware of what was taking place, but no one knew at that time the full extent of Earl's mental health.

Brother Russ, on his way to give assistance, met Earl walking on the road from his home with baby Beverly wrapped in a blanket and carried under his arm. Russ coaxed Earl to place the baby on the seat and come with him while he had the baby checked out at the hospital.

I cannot imagine how the next pieces come together but Russ handed the baby to the hospital staff and told them to call the police for Earl. Then he left to find Mom, believing that she was in danger.

By this time, Uncle Bill had returned to Earl's home. It was then that they found Mom and Delores. They had been strangled.

The police arrived. They had been called by Delores three times previously. She had told them that she was afraid for her life. She didn't have a phone and had to walk to a neighbour's house to make the call. According to what the family know, she was told to get Earl to the hospital.

Earl was initially charged with two counts of murder. Later, it was determined he was criminally insane, and he was committed to Oliver mental hospital in Edmonton.

Earl was diagnosed with paranoid schizophrenia. He would receive treatment for this disorder. Although he would be released into the community over the years, he was unable to be rehabilitated. Earl passed away at Oliver mental hospital from an unrelated illness several years later.

Meanwhile, Mom's apartment in Ponoka had to be looked after, there was a funeral to be arranged, and living arrangements for Gordie had to be discussed.

We held a double funeral and Mom and Delores were buried beside each other at the Edgerton Cemetery.

Gordie went to live with Roger. He was enrolled for a short time at the high school in Hardisty before leaving to enter the workforce where he became a welder.

Earl's four children went to reside with their maternal grandmother and later were taken into foster care.

Our family spent may years recovering from our grief as we supported each other and carried on with life. We were very angry that the police did not respond when Delores called to express her fear.

Initially people encouraged us to sue the police. We discussed it and as a family we decided that would not be what Mom would have wanted us to do. We found strength in our belief that out of this incident would come change in how the police would respond to women calling them for support in dangerous situations. I am sad to say this has not been the case and there are still women dying because the police refuse to respond to dangerous situations unless or until there is an actual incident occurring.

Police Charge Husband

An Edmonton woman called police Thursday to say her husband was dangerous and likely to commit a crime. A few hours later, she and her mother-in-law were dead by strangulation in their northeast city home.

Earl Walter Lehr, 29, the father of four children, has been charged with capital murder in the death of his wife and his mother, who adopted him as a small child.

The man's 26-year-old wife Delores, of 12820 52nd St., and his mother, Mrs. Dion Lehr, were found dead by members of the family.

Police today investigated a report that Lehr's wife had called them Thursday saying he was dangerous and likely to commit a crime.

Murder
(Continued from Page 1)

fully throughout the house seeking clues and bits of evidence.

FIRST THOUGH SHOT

Initial reports of the deaths indicated the women had been shot. However, police entered the home and found the bodies of the women in a bedroom. There were no indications a gun had been used. Both bodies were taken to the morgue at the Royal Alexandra for autopsies.

Lehr's mother came to Alberta from Leven, Sask. several years ago. She taught grade one classes at the Edgerton elementary school for more than 10 years. She had also taught at the Hutterite colony near Irma.

Mrs. Lehr's husband, Jack, died about two years ago. She had five other children, in addition to Earl. Two married sons, Donald and Russel, live in Edmonton. A third married son, Roger, lives at Hardisty. The fourth son, Gordon, attends high school at Camrose. A married daughter, Doris Wakefield, lives at Wainwright. Roger formerly played hockey with the Edmonton Oil Kings.

Mrs. Lehr attended summer school this year and was to teach high school at Ponoka.

A police report

Funeral Services For Mrs. E. Lehr And Mrs. D. Lehr

Rev. Gordon Ingram, assisted by Rev. Brian Brown, conducted a double funeral service for the late Mrs. Edith Dion Lehr and the late Mrs. Mary Delores Lehr. Following the service they were laid to rest in the Edgerton Cemetery.

Mrs. Edith Lehr leaves to mourn her loss her children, Donald and Russell of Edmonton, Roger and Gordon of Hardisty, and Doris (Mrs. Chas. Wakefield) of Wainwright; also nine grandchildren; two brothers, Bill and Arthur Cross; and one sister, Mrs. Mary Kergan. Pallbearers were Mr. Ken Bedford, Mr. George Sawyer, Mr. Len Burton, Mr. Tom Withnell Sr., Mr. Oliver Griffiths and Mr. John Ronjom.

Mrs. Delores Lehr leaves her four children, Sharon 8, Edith 6, Martha Jean 4, and Herb 3. Also her parents, Mr. and Mrs. P. Fayant of Fishing Lake, Alberta; and seven brothers and five sisters. Pallbearers were Mr. Dud Sawyer, Mr. Fritz Alwood, Mr. John Harvard, Mr. Paul Belik, Mr. Don Guy and Mr. Don Mills.

Beautiful floral tributes were received from: The Lehr Family; The Fayant Family; Arthur, Bill and Mary and Families; Mr. and Mrs. Gilbert Fayant; Mr. and Mrs. Paul Portrus; The

Funeral

We constantly got together almost in a clinging fashion just to be together as much as possible. None of us received the grief counselling that we could have benefited from. Just as mental health services weren't available for Earl as he was growing up, it was still an uncharted area for families in crisis and difficult to obtain in 1962.

When we got together, we did not discuss Mom's death. We partied and laughed and shoved the memories down deep. We instinctively knew that Mom would want us to carry on and make the best possible lives for ourselves.

We lived in a community where our family was well known, and the circumstances of our loss were well known. Because of this public awareness, our tragedy was not something we talked about. It wasn't until many years later that I have been able to discuss the tragedy our family experienced.

Some of the pain has dispersed over the years, but the memory of our loving mother never dies.

Bachelor of education. A Bachelor of Education Degree was issued posthumously at Fall convocation in 1962.

Although Mom's Normal school training qualified her to teach in Saskatchewan in 1930, it wasn't recognized in full by Alberta's Department of Education. Therefore, she was required to upgrade and be in possession of a Bachelor of Education degree in order to continue teaching. She was able to negotiate this through regular attendance at summer school at University of Alberta.

On August 30th, 1962, Dione met with her maker and began her life in Eternity.

Graduation picture
Our mom Edith Dione Cross

About The Author

This book is Doris Wakefield's first published material. She has always been interesting in writing and would often read late into the night. She first started writing while she was in high school, and when her children were small decided to take a journalism course. Her belief in God's love and goodness is her strength and continues to influence her love of family and community.

As a child growing up on the farm in Saskatchewan, she played with her dolls and dreamed of having a large family of her own someday. Doris was married to her teen age sweetheart, Charlie for 52 years and together raised a family of six children. Their family has grown to include the blessing of grandchildren and great grandchildren.

Doris credits her greatest influences to her Mother, Dione, her Grandmother Cecelia and her Aunt Mary as well as her husband Charlie.

Doris considers herself a learner, a dreamer and a doer. Her journey through life has seen her return to education as an adult to obtain her Diploma in Social Work. For many years she has been actively involved in community service and work with services for the disabled. Doris has recently returned to the community where she and Charlie raised their family and is enjoying her senior years.

www.ingramcontent.com/pod-product-compliance
Lightning Source LLC
LaVergne TN
LVHW041650060526
838200LV00040B/1788